Perpetual Direct Democracy

Ion Delsol

ISBN:1466420995

ISBN-13: **978-1466420991**

DEDICATION

To all those who are ready for a social change and are willing to try an egalitarian, nonviolent, and leaderless political system.

Table of Contents:

FOREWORD

by: Linda J.Taffs

A tool for social change in our life time: "Perpetual Direct Democracy"

Ion Delsol challenges that ion of the sun in each one of us to step out of the traditional political system which empowers not citizens but representative leaders and political parties for "temporal dictatorships."

Canadian representative-democracy has served us well for 145 years. This booklet goes beyond representative-democracy, advancing towards the next step in the evolution of democracy. The simple yet profound hypothesis int this booklet suggests a monumental political shift from the traditional representative-democracy into Perpetual Direct Democracy, PDD.

It starts by addressing the obvious question: Why Does Perpetual Direct Democracy Matter Now? In other words, why was it not technologically possible fifty years ago?, It also explores the possibility that we might have reached the ideological maturity and appetite for political change, at this time.

To examine those questions; the following chapter defines some factors and perspectives of democracy which are relevant to this discussion; and because PDD is all about referendums, it includes a list of relevant referendums that have taken place in Canada.

To confirm the need for a political change, the PDD booklet cites some factual disconnections between the Canadian government and its citizens. It not only shows the political disfunction, but it suggests a solution through the creation of a constitution for a federation of sovereign states or provinces within a New Canada.

The central message in the last two chapters is that, in order to gain sovereignty, we must assume the responsibility of legislating our own constitutional statutes, laws, and regulations.

It says that, the social change, most of us want, may be realized more effectively by ourselves with a PDD system than by empowering political leaders and hierarchical political parties.

"All tyranny needs to gain a foothold is for people of good conscience to remain silent."

Thomas Jefferson

CHAPTER 1

Why does Perpetual Direct Democracy, PDD, Matters Now?

1.1 - The sooner a significant number of us, the citizens, realize our right to legislate our own laws, and to establish them into a "Citizens' Constitution", the sooner a more egalitarian distribution of goods and services we will have, a more sustainable harvesting of resources we will manage, and a more peaceful world we will live in.

1.2 - The most popular tool of democracy up to now has been the right to protest the disconnect between governments and its citizens. Citizens, all over the world, have been protesting far too long. Although protests generate some degree of publicity, solidarity, and personal satisfaction, protests are seldom successful. Frustratingly, public protests are often ignored, politely heard, or at worst, violently squashed by repressive governments. Michael Nagler in his book, "In Search for a Nonviolent Future" says: "The tail of protesting wrongs would never wag the dog of building a society."

1.3 - The essencial factors of why PDD matters now are that the time has come when we are technologically and intellectually ready to go beyond protesting. We are ready to take the next step towards developing an ongoing, participatory governance, or Perpetual direct democracy, PDD.

1.4 - Now is the time, because unprecedented internet technology enables us to be abundantly informed about relevant social issues. Now polling with the latest computer technology, as never before in history, has made it easy for us to participate in instant plebiscites, tabulate public opinion, and potentially legislate the people's agenda within a new Citizens' Constitution, as expanded on chapter 9.

1.5 - Additional to technological advances, we have learned from history, and experienced in our life time how legislative power concentrated in the hands of monarchs, dictators, or a few politicians has inherently corrupted in the past, and potentially will continue to corrupt in the future. Also, Unnecessarily empowered representatives, become increasingly vulnerable to being co-opted, or coerced by economic interests. For this reason, political decision-making-power should not be concentrated on the hands of just a few selected representatives, but it should be decentralized and left in the hands of all citizens.

Baron Acton (1834 - 1902)

"Power corrupts;

absolute power corrupts absolutely".

1.6 - The current Representative Democracy, inherited from the hierarchical tradition of parliamentary monarchies, has served its time, but in spite of the technological advances and political maturity of the citizens, democracy has stagnated technologically and is no longer politically correct. Democracy today can and should be expanded to include all citizens sharing equal political power of one person, one vote on all significant political decisions.

1.7 - The present electoral tradition of granting a term of office is flawed mainly because it is too easy for many of us to be fooled by propaganda, during the relatively short period of elections, leaving us to suffer the consequence of often wrong decision for several years. Adopting PDD would make it more difficult for all of us to be mislead, by a few for-profit propagandists and lobbyists.

"You can fool some of the people all of the time, and all of the people some of the time, but you can not fool all of the people all of the time".

Abraham Lincoln   1809 – 1865
16th U.S. president

1.8 - Countries which seriously want social change, like, Venezuela, Ecuador, and Iceland, start the change by rewiriting their constitution.

Thomas Jefferson, (1743-1826) draftsman of the Declaration of Independence and Founding Father of the United States, said that the constitution should be rewritten every 19 years.

We do not need to literally restrict constitutional changes to the term of 19 years, but we can figuratively interprete it as our perpetual responsibility of amending our constitution as often as needed, so each generation should define for itself how it should be governed

1.9 - In summary, If we are ready to take full responsibility of our political choices, now is the time. We are living in an age when the best communications technology can enable us to adopt PDD. We can now legislate our own rules for an egalitarian distribution of our commonwealth; we can legislate and practice the most environmentally sustainable laws; and we can transform our War Economy into Peace Economy.

When a multitude of us are willing and able to make political decisions through a PDD system, we will effectively change and optimize our social system. We can potentially develop the best possible standard of living, that ever existed, for all humanity.

Shakyamuni Buddha

is in the Here and Now

CHAPTER 2

Factors and Perspectives of Democracy.

2.1 - The idea of democracy may be looked at from many perspectives. It has been used and misused as an excuse to occupy other countries, to overthrow governments, and to exert, sometimes benevolent, but often repressive authority. Here are a few perspectives of democracy relevant to this PDD thesis.

2.2 - Inclusion

Electoral inclusivity in many nations has gradually evolved to equality. That is, one person - one vote, extended to all races, genders, religious affiliations, and economic classes. These gains in inclusivity need to be recognized and celebrated as a positive evolution, and as fundamental factors in democracy.

Universal male suffrage in France, following the French Revolution of 1848.

2.3 - Representative Democracy

Representative democracy means that the power to legislate the rules of governance is transferred to a few political representatives. This hierarchical concession of power has been entrenched in our political culture by inertia as an old sacred tradition. In fact, power continues to be dictated from the top down because citizens, obliviously of their own volition, continue to give away, what should be, their right to legislate their own rules.

"the most effective way to restrict democracy is to transfer decision making from the public arena to unaccountable institutions: kings and princes priestly casters, military juntas, party dictatorships, or modern corporations."   Noam Chomsky.

2.4 - Term of Office and Recall

We must also consider the legal limitations to political participation we assume during a "term of office". In essence, the only time when political power flows from the bottom-up is on election day when all citizens are allowed to endorse their political power to a political representative. This means, citizens' decision-making power is permitted only once every three or four years. In other words, the citizens' democratic right to make a single decision is restricted to less than one day out of more than a thousand days. Term-of-office gives political supremacy to political representatives, and legally constitutes a temporal dictatorship. This one day democracy is the main sources of political abuse, public frustration and peoples's cynicism.

During the 90's, Stephen Harper and the Reform Party stood for citizens's initiative, referendums, and recall, but most Canadians were not ready for this idealism, so an alliance between the

Conservative Party and our traditional representative democracy, with a term-of-office, got Harper into power. Recall legislation is no longer in his agenda.

2.5 - Separation of Powers.

We have inherited from Ancient Greece and the Roman Republic, the governance model "trias politica", or the separation of three political powers: Legislative, Executive, and Judicial.

The blending of the three powers is the parliamentary-monarchies' choice, and the separation of powers is the republican's choice. However, legislative, judicial, and governance practices vary from country to country, according to their perception and trust of "checks and balances".

In Canada a few elected legislators, leading the political party with the most elected representatives, automatically become the executive government. Additionally, this small cadre of politicians assumes the authority to appoint their choice of supreme court judges and Senators. This blending of powers concentrates unaccountable political authority, prone to abuse, into the hands of the Prime Minister's Office and a few Cabinet Ministers.

In the U.S.A. the separation of powers creates some struggles between the executive office of the President, and the legislative bodies of Congress and Senate. However, the office of the President having the power to veto some legislation, and select Supreme Court judges, also concentrates legislative, executive, and judicial power in its hands, and potentially it becomes prone to fascism or plutocracy disguised as democracy.

2.6 - Media, Information and Propaganda.

Media is an indispensable factor in democracy because rational decision making emanates from a well informed population. Media can be used as an effective tool for factual information, or it can be misused as a detrimental lever for propaganda. Commercial media, owned and operated by a small but wealthy elite, advertises and sponsors their political representatives. Once elected, political representatives, indebted to their financiers, will inevitably lobby for their sponsors' agenda.

This skewing of democracy has been described by the book : "Manufacturing Consent" where Chomsky and Herman explain that corporate media, as profit-driven institutions, tend to serve and further the agendas of the interests of dominant, elite groups in our society.

2.7 - Economic interests, hiring advertising experts to manipulate public opinion through the media, have historically misinformed the people and created the illusion that we are the good people and there is a bad, evil enemy out there, therefore, they argue, it is our humanitarian responsibility to destroy it.

For example, the "weapons of mass destruction" propaganda used in 2002 by U.S. politicians to invade and occupy Iraq in 2003, instigated public support to attack an illusionary enemy.

This phenomenon is explained by Greg Palast in his book "The Best Democracy Money Can Buy".

2.8 - Majority Rule is constituted by a conventional agreement. Sometimes it has no predetermined threshold, as in "First Past The Post", where the candidate with the highest number of votes wins. Other times a simple majority of more than half carries the motion. However, on issues dimmed very important, a "Supermajority Rule" of two-thirds, three-quarters, or more is required to carry the motion. The majority should always consider and accommodate, as much as possible, the concerns of the minority.

Jean-Jacques Rousseau

1712 – 1778 advocated the use of supermajority voting on important decisions when he said, "The more the deliberations are important and serious, the more the opinion that carries should approach unanimity."

2.9 - A hybrid blend of representative democracy and direct democracy has been introduced in twenty six of the United States of America, and at least seven Canadian Provinces have had plebiscites and referendums. However, the real transition from representative democracy to direct democracy has been stagnating for a long time as if it were a utopia. Only cosmetic changes have been promoted as diversion and tokenism of direct democracy.

The reason for this impasse is clearly explained by the Former Leader of the Liberal Party of BC Gordon Gibson. As he put it, change will not happen easily, because the gate keepers, with the power  to make this political change, are the same politicians who would lose their political power if real changes were to be made.

Having looked at several perspectives and component of democracy, and having explored how democracy can be subverted or co-opted by business' interests, let us review some historical plebiscites and referendums, as possible precursors of PDD.

CHAPTER 3

Some Relevant Referendums in Canada.

3.1 - Plebiscites and referendum have been around for over a hundred years. A non-binding plebiscite on prohibition of alcohol was held in Canada on September 29, 1898

3.2 - The Province of British Columbia introduced The Direct Legislation Bill in 1919. J. S. Cowper, MLA defended the proposed law. The Bill was passed, but never received Royal Assent. The government feared that it would be ruled unconstitutional.

3.3 - A non-binding plebiscite on conscription was held in Canada on April 27, 1942.

3.4 - The National Referendum on the Charlottetown Accord was a package of proposed amendments to the Constitution of Canada by the Conservative government of Brian Mulroney. The referendum was defeated on October 26, 1992.

3.5 - The Block Quebecois referendum on October 30th. 1995, Lead by Gilles Duceppe, asked whether Quebec should secede from Canada and become an independent state. The motion was defeated by a very narrow margin.

3.6 - In The October 17, 1991 British Columbia Recall and Initiative Referendum, Rita Johnson, in concession to Mel Couvelier's initiative, asked two questions: One on whether elected officials should be subject to be recalled and another on whether voters should be given the right to initiate legislation by referendum. Both questions were decisively approved by the electorate with 83% and 85% respectively.

In theory, the Initiative and Recall Legislation was introduced by Ujjal Dosanjh to the BC Legislature in 1996 as law. In practice however, the requirements for recalling MLAs were deliberately onerous, so that although many ridings started the petition, none were qualified to trigger a Recall by-election during the following 16 years.

NDP politicians of the 90's, when asked why the "Recall" requirements were so cumbersome, replied that they did not believe in Recalling politicians.

3.7 - A referendum on electoral reform was held on May 17, 2005. British Columbian voters were asked to approve a new electoral system based on the Single Transferable Vote, STV-BC. It failed to meet the required "supermajority" threshold of 60%. A second referendum on the same issue was held on May 12, 2009. The second defeat meant a "supermajority" of 60.92% voting for retaining the current "first past the post" electoral system.

3.8 - In Rossland, BC, referenda was adopted and practiced, between 1991 and 2001, until the local government was made aware, by the BC Minister of Municipal Affairs, of the "ultra virus" illegality of it.

In Canada, a referendum, meaning a binding vote in which an entire electorate is asked to either accept or reject a particular law, needs the adoption of a constitutional amendment. Currently, the supreme authority to legislate comes down from the Queen to parliament, not from the people up to politicians. Andre Carrel, a retired city manager, expands on this issue in his book, "Citizens' Hall."

3.9 - Elections BC administered the HST (Harmonized Sales Tax) Mail-in Referendum – June 13 – August 5, 2011.

Former Premier of BC Bill Van der Zalm , and 54% of voters rejected the g o v e r n m e n t 's imposed HST.

The point in this chapter is not to a n a l y z e   w h i c h form of taxation is more fair, or who benefits most from either form of taxation. The important issue, here is to show that the citizens of BC have been allowed to make a binding, budgetary decision which is different from the government's decision.

This list of plebiscites and referendums is just a historical sample of the precedence and local experimentation of citizens participation. It demonstrates that direct democracy is possible.

The next chapter focuses on some detrimental contradictions between the few leaders in government and the majority of Canadian citizens.

CHAPTER 4

Citizens' Vision in Discord with Governments' Policies.

4.1 - Dissatisfaction with our governments' agenda, and protesting against government policies will continue to happen, as long as we continue to subordinate, or give away, our decision making power to political representatives. Perpetual Direct Democracy as proposed in Chapter six, is a possible solution. In this chapter we highlight a few instances where governments are clearly marching to a different tune than the peoples' aspirations.

4.2 - There is a lingering question in the minds of many Canadians since the 1988 Free Trade Agreement, FTA, was discussed. This decision, was probably not the choice of the majority of Canadians, but it was legally the choice of the political party with the most representatives.
January 1, 1994 the North American Free Trade Agreement - NAFTA, came into force, superseding FTA. Again, this controversial agreement was mandated without meaningful information,  public discussion, or approval by the people.

In stead of having a referendum which might legitimize the agreements, or require their cancelation, the Canadian government is discussing the North American Security and Prosperity Partnership, NASPP, and the Comprehensive Economic and Trade Agreement, CETA, between Canada and the European Union. These negotiations between high level political representatives and business representatives exclude the 99% of citizens' opinions and concerns. These negotiations lack transparency, public discussion, and approval of the people by referendum.

4.3 - Military Interventions into foreign countries are serious life and death issue, yet only a few executive ministers and a few political representatives are authorized, by us, to decide, even against the wish of most of us.

Since 2001, year after year the polls have shown public rejection to the Canadian military intervention in Afghanistan. According to an Angus Reid poll - February 2011, 63%  of Canadians oppose the war in Afghanistan. Yet the Canadian military were directed to fighting to death in Afghanistan, for about 10 years, and continue their condescending presence in Afghanistan under the NATO pretense of "humanitarian intervention".

4.4 - Foreign Policy.

The diplomatic, trade, and aid policies, of the Canadian government, often are not consistent with the wishes of the majority of citizens. Canada's unconditional support of foreign governments, specially nations which are in violation of UN resolutions, is constantly being questioned to no avail by human rights and peace activists. Religious prejudices, ethnic preferences, or the economic investment and trade privileges to some countries at the expense of less privileged nations might not be the ethical priority to most Canadians.

PALESTINIAN LOSS OF LAND 1946 TO 2011

After carefully observing the Charter of Human Rights and Freedoms, and international laws, we would benefit by having a referendum on all issues of foreign policy rather than allowing a few political leaders make unwanted foreign policies in our name.

4.5 - Bank of Canada.

Since 1986, the Committee on Monetary and Economic Reform, COMER, has been advocating for the Bank of Canada to assume its original mandate of lending money to all levels of government.

Comer.org and Paul Hellyer, former Defence Minister and founder of the Canadian Action Party of Canada, claimed that over $60 billion in yearly interest on all levels of government debts combined, paid to investors, could instead finance an optimal health care  system, tuition free post secondary education, and sufficient social housing for all Canadians.

The Bank of Canada, apparently being subverted by the for-profit financial system, needs to be, understood, and restored to its original mandate of lending money to all levels of government.
The current banking policy generously benefits financial investors at the expense of all Canadians.

4.6 - Health Care System.

Most Canadians and the BC Health Coalition believe that Health Care is a human right - everyone should be able to count on high quality, universal and comprehensive health care which is publicly funded by taxes, and operated by public servants.

Yet, federal and provincial governments have been eroding the public health care system, making it vulnerable to privatization. This is an obvious disconnect between governments enabling for-profit businesses and people needing not for profit health care services.

4.7 - Education System.

The United Public Education, UPE, a non-partisan coalition of student unions, teacher associations and other groups who represent every level of education in BC, Canada, raises awareness about the chronic underfunding of the public education system.

Rather than collecting the needed share of taxes from those who can afford, governments create deficits to justify the reduction of services claiming that the lack of funds, from uncollected taxes, is a natural scarcity of money.

4.8 - Social Housing.

The federal and provincial governments in Canada developed legislation in the 1970s providing financing for Social Housing through

the Canada Mortgage and Housing Corporation, CHMC. However, political will dissipated in the 1990s, the governments reduced the funds available for mortgages, and eliminated the start up funding for cooperatives.

A significant number of the working poor, who pay more than 50% of their income on shelter, would welcome a public discussion and referendum about building sufficient social housing.

4.9 - Department of Defence of Canada

Conservative reports of the National Defence Budget, currently decided by very few politicians, shows an increase from $15 billion in 2006 to $20 billion in 2011. Meanwhile,

health care, education and housing costs are being gradually shifted from general tax revenues to individuals as fees-per-service. Such ideological budget shifts should be clearly explained, publicly discussed, and universally decided by referendum.

This list of political issues illustrates and confirms the imminent need to shift from being governed by legislation created by a few politicians, as we do under Representative Democracy, to being governed by the citizens' own legislation, as it would be under "Perpetual Direct Democracy", PDD.

In the next chapter we look at the current political ideologies and systems of governance in Canada.

CHAPTER 5

Current Ideologies and Systems of Governance.

5.1 - The Story of "Mouse-land" as told by Tommy Douglas in 1944, is still relevant today. He suggested that mice, by switching their vote from: a white cat, to a black cat, to a grey cat, did not improve their lot. The trouble wasn't with the colour of the cats. The trouble was that they were cats, and cats naturally look after their own interests. Projecting this anecdote to our era, 2012; switching our vote from one party to another party, for the past 145 years in Canada, has not served the best interest of most people. The trouble has not been the ideological intention of the parties, which is always altruistic during elections. The trouble is that all parties need to hoard the most power, if they want to dictate their own agenda to us.

Tommy Douglas suggested that the mice should elect, not cats of any colour, but their own fellow mice to office.

Advancing that thought further, we suggest that, if all the citizens were the mice, we all would become our own legislators instead of giving our political power away to cats, of any party. Party labels do not always represent their party ideologies, and electoral discourses may not always be practiced once the party is in power. Let us look at some of the most prominent political ideologies in Canada.

5.2 - One the largest political forces in Canada, 25% strong as of the 2011 elections, is the conservative ideology. This label is not necessarily synonymous with conserving the environment, but is primarily focused on conserving the economic status-quo of maximizing profits.

This hierarchical ideology benefits, above all, financial investors and private property owners.

Under this ideology, the cyclical economic success of the working class becomes dependent on paid employment and on the market economy.

Conservative ideology also appears beneficial to the majority of citizens who become dependent on the trickle down economy. However, that hierarchical, success is cyclical and based on the exploitation of labour, the swindling of the commonwealth, and the ravishing of natural resources from around the world.

5.3 - Another main political force is the progressive-liberal ideology which is based on balancing individual freedoms and the collective good resulting in a mixed economy. Liberal ideology, in principle, is neither monolithic "right" nor revolutionary "left", but pragmatic "centre". The liberalization of economic, religious and cultural rights is a compelling ideology.

However, because of the current political system, of representative democracy, legislation is influenced first by the personal bias of the few elected politicians, rather than by the will of most people; and second, the progressive liberal intention gets tilted towards the dictates of the corporate lobby which are generally in conflict with the collective good.

5.4 - The New Democratic Party, NDP, similar to the progressive liberal ideology predicates a balance of justice between individual property rights and the commonwealth. In other words, a balance between socialism and capitalism, as practiced in most Northern European countries.

NDP's ideology, similar to that of the social minded liberals, is often lost under the political representative's individual bias, the organized labour and business' interests who support the party, and the Party's main drive to gain power.

5.5 - The Green Party is an environmental movement of conservatives, liberals and socialists, singularly concerned with the ecological survival of our planet. Because of the Greens' multilateral diagnosis of environmental concerns, the Green agenda, to alleviate the ecological symptoms, needs to include all ideological-isms: "green-blue" capitalism, "green-red" liberalism, as well as "green-orange" NDP'ism.

5.6 - In the field of electoral reform, in order to have multiple representatives per riding, all shades of blue, red and orange political persuasions have considered *enlarging the areas of political ridings*. This change, claiming to bring more democracy, was twice proposed by STV-BC, on the referendums of 2005 and 2009, and it was twice defeated.

5.7 - All political parties, also aiming at advancing democracy, have tried the exact opposite change, that is, *reducing the at-large municipal areas,* represented by multiple councilors, into smaller wards, represented by a single councillor. Legislation to this effect was put to a referendum and also failed in Vancouver in 2004.

5.8 - NDPs and Greens have considered empowering their parties according to their proportional overall (at large) vote. This would imply appointing, if necessary, a number of unelected party member to replace a number of elected politicians in some local ridings in order to comply with the (at large) party-proportionality. This reform is exactly the opposite to the city's "wards proposition" for more local representation. A Citizen's initiative to this electoral reform, failed to collect 10% of electoral support, as required by the BC's electoral system, in 2001.

5.9 - To transcend changing political parties from blue to red to orange to green, like in Tommy Douglas' anecdote, we need to clearly identify our individual and collective priorities, independent of hierarchical political parities.

Identifying and building consensus on PDD ideology is the topic of the next chapter.

CHAPTER 6

Perpetual Direct Democracy, "PDD": a New Ideology

6.1 - Perpetual Direct Democracy.

Democracy, in principle, is not a new idea. It has been understood as a political power "from the people, by the people, for the people" since ancient Greece to the American Constitution. For over two thousand years democracy has evolved, in most nations.

It starts as an exclusive right for property owning men, and evolves into a universal membership including all men and women of all races, in most nations.

What is new in PDD is that it advances the evolution of democracy, this time shifting the political power from the traditional representative democracy, "RD" to all the citizens: directly and perpetually. This two new factors make PDD a relatively new system.

6.2 - Reassigning Political Responsibility.

So far we have seen how, in the current RD, citizens' decision making is allowed only one day out of more than a thousand days. PDD means to reclaim the citizens' right to have every day as citizens' decision making day, not just on election day.

6.3 - Our responsibility to keep political power.

We looked in chapter four, how disconnected the RD elite has been from most of us. However, the purpose of PDD is not just to show our mistake of giving away our political decision making power, to a representative leaders, but PDD means to reclaim the right, the confidence, the ability and the responsibility of all citizens to make all relevant political decisions directly and perpetually.

PDD reveals that our perennial disfunction with government elites, which engage in unwanted wars, erode social services, and mismanage natural resources, is in fact the product of our own misunderstanding about our legal commitment to RD on election day. PDD ideology means that we the citizens, do not give away that political power to make desicions, but hold on to it so we can legislate our own rules.

6.4 - Electing Executive Administrators.

The PDD thesis proposes a system where we will no longer need to elect political leaders like City Councellors, MLAs or MPs. Instead, we will only elect executive administrators for each city department, State Executive Ministers to replace the current Members of the Legislative Assembly, and Executive Federal Co-ministers for each ministry to replace the current Members of Parliament. These executive administrators, Ministers, and Co-Ministers would be perpetually accountable and subordinate to our right to recall them anytime.

6.5 - Trusting Human Nature.

We, the proponents of PDD, optimistically assume that the referendum system will overwhelmingly show a majority of citizens wanting to develop and participate in an egalitarian society.

We also assume that the PDD system will show a cooperative rather than a competitive driving force for our activities.

In other words, we assume that most people want to build a society where the competitive market economy is no longer the driving force of our policies and activities, and that a fair allocation of natural and human resources becomes possible by contributing according to people's abilities and distributing according to people's needs.

Finally, we expect that the majority of people will happily legislate and comply with ethnic, religious, and gender human rights granted to all minorities.

6.6 - Fundamental Human Values.

Hopefully, PDD will reflect the most fundamental human values of empathy, equality, justice, security, and ecological conservation.

Empathy:

Understandably, empathy by itself can not be legislated; however, Laws and empathy are indispensable and complementary. Law without empathy is a despotic body. Empathy without laws is a spirit without a body.

For thousands of years, the concept of love has been predicated by Jesus, Tolstoy, Gandhi. and many others who understood empathy, as the spirit of the law and a fundamental element in human relations and survival.

Michel Nagler in his book, "In search for a Nonviolent Future" says that we need to change ourselves, our thoughts, our words, and our deeds in order to change the world.

Equality:

Adopting racial, cultural, and economic equal rights will free us from hierarchy, exploitation, and oppression. Epidemiologist Richard Wilkinson, in his book "The Spirit Level", shows how detrimental inequality is to all of us, and why equality is better for everyone.

Christian Andersen illustrated this cultural idolatry of hierarchy and inequality in his 1837 Fairy Tale, "The Emperor Has No Clothes."

Justice and Security:

Security and Justice of one is the security and justice of all. Security is a mutual fairness in human relations, rather than on the culture of fear, punishment, and retaliation. According to Professor Wilkinson, the more egalitarian a social system is, the less crime it breathes. So, security is directly proportional to economic justice for all.

Ecological justice: Buddhist teachings and native Americans tell us that if we see ourselves as separate beings, unconnected with each other and with the environment, we will eventually destroy the ecosystem and ourselves with it.

6.7 - Peoples' Legislation.

PDD means to register, discuss, and quantify the mission, statutes, and laws based on an ideological balance between individual liberties and collective freedoms. The results of these registered initiatives, voluntary discussed for a reasonable length of time, and counted on an on-going referendum, will become the peoples' choice from the ground up, rather than legislation imposed from the government elite down.

6.8 - A Nonviolent Evolution.

Although PDD is a radical change, the shifting process from RD to PDD, does not need to be chaotic, abrupt or violent. PDD appeals to the matureness of citizens to gradually develop the new system in nonviolence, as a natural evolution of democracy.

6.9 - Identifying the peoples' agenda.

After a conscious realization of our sovereignty from hierarchical politics, the most fundamental step is to clearly define the people's agenda and write it down into a citizens constitution.

CHAPTER 7

So, what can we do about it?

7.1 Build a new system rather than protest the old.

Even if it takes time away from reactionary protests on single issues, let's organize with the clear intention of building not just political parties or political movements, but to develop the peoples' ability to register their specific initiatives, and tabulate the consensus on plebiscites. The results of this public plebiscites would be discussed and confirmed by binding referendums to ultimately legislate the values of universal fairness, equality, responsibility, freedom and security.

When a significant number of us adopt PDD as a viable political system, we may decide to create a phantom government, parallel and supplementary to the existing one.

The Albert Einstein Institution promotes Dr. Gene Sharp's Methods of Nonviolent Political Action; one of which is: "Dual sovereignty and parallel government." (Boston: Porter Sargent Publishers, 1973)

7.2 - Co-create Laws with Empathic Intentionality.

To upgrade the current social system, we need to periodically envision and re-develop our procedural framework, our laws. A new political system must be based on a philosophical, humane, ethical, and egalitarian intention.

Empathic intentionality can not be created and dictated by well meaning individuals or benevolent governments. Laws with empathic intentionality must be collectively initiated and mutually consented by all citizens.

Vladimir Lenin, Mao Zedong, Josip Broz Tito, Saddam Hussein, Muammar al-Gaddafi, and many other dictators had a good paternalistic intention to help their people, and they were temporarely successful in implementing a good standad of living for their countries, but because the good intended laws were ruthlessly dictated and enforced from the top of centralized piramids of power, the masses at the base of the piramid suffered human rights abuses inherent in all undemocratic, hierarchical systems of governance.

So, the systemic environment of laws and governance must be generated from people's initiatives, not from political leaders. PDD will reciprocally influence our individual and collective behavior.

"A world worthy of humanity cannot be created through the state." John Holloway.

7.3 - **Review our Sense of Equality**

A basic requirement to this political transformation is the citizens' conscious realization of equality and sovereignty, independent from hierarchical political structures.

We need to recognize the innate equality in all human beings. We need to realize and dispel the mythological belief in the superiority/inferiority complex, entrenched deeply in our culture.

This delusion is apparent in our admiration for monarchs, arts and sports celebrities, religious and political leaders. This emotional propensity to idolize individuals, generates tribal affiliations and loyalties to crowds of followers rather than fosters independent rational thinking.

When we rely on benevolent dictators or philanthropic magnates to provide for better social services, without questioning the source of their power or wealth, we underestimate and undermine our own abilities.

In fact, leaders are not any wiser in making political decisions for the collective good. We have seen throughout history highly educated and intelligent individuals execute horrendous crimes to humanity by enabling wars and civil coercion. Yet, people continue to admire, trust, and empower leaders as if they were super humans or deities.

We must prevent our rational thinking from getting overwhelmed by our emotional admiration of charismatic personalities. We need to challenge and overcome this cultural mythology. We need to rethink and rebuild our sense of equality.

7.4 - **Replace Coercion with Consensus**

Democracy can not be established by the tyranny of the majority. The will of the majority must respect and accommodate, as far as possible, the wishes, needs and human rights of minorities.

Although democracy and violence are interrelated forces which determine the outcome of human interactions, we must remember the popular misnomer that WW1 was violently fought to end all wars, this popular belief has repeatedly failed in the past hundred years. Wars violently impose temporary social order, but do not bring social justice and peace.

Mahatma Gandhi said: " I object to violence because when it appears to do good, the good is only temporary, the evil it does is permanent."

A few countries, less economically and technologically developed than Canada, have established a Ministry of Peace, with the purpose of developing methods and training student-brigades for nonviolent solutions for conflicts.

We need to learn to solve our conflicts within ourselves and with other nation in a nonviolent approach. We need to replace the misnomered "Humanitarian Intervention" mission of our current Ministry of Defense with a mission of a Ministry of Peace, similar to the one introduced in 2012 in the Canadian Parliament as Bill C-373

7.5 - **Overcome The Enemy Syndrome**.

We need to overcome the perception of separation between them and us. Them, meaning other nations or our own oppressive government. On the other hand us, meaning the oppressed, defenseless civilians. We must stop blaming our elected rulers for our own political acquiescence or apathy.

It is our responsibility to stop following, acquiescing, and merely protesting the current hierarchical system and business agenda; and start building our own system because ultimately, we are the makers and consumers of superfluous and toxic goods and services, and ultimately, here in Canada, we the people elect the very politician whom we later blame.

"We participate in the breaking of our own doing, the construction of our own subordination."
John Holloway.

As the Pogo Papers described it in 1953:

"We have met the enemy, and he is us."

7.6 - **Conserve The Good and Toss The Bad**.

Current laws and government regulations which efficiently distribute goods and services according to need, must be conserved and perhaps enhanced. However, laws which prioritize for-profit businesses, by giving them personhood status, at the expense and detriment of exploited citizens, must be fixed immediately.

We must also give credit and remember with empathy that our influential predecessors created the various political systems and laws with the good intention of organizing our social system. This was created according to the culture and political understanding of their time.

Times and technology have evolved, so we need to graciously upgrade the traditional, hierarchical political ideology of representative democracy into the new PDD.

7.7 - **Shift from Competitiveness to Cooperation.**

We need to challenge the prevalent importance given to the for-profit-businesses based on the competitiveness of the market economy, as if consumerism and economic competitiveness were the driving force of human activities.

When we transcend the competitive agenda, and it's propagandized culture, we will realize that a fair distribution of human resources through cooperation is the most civilized motivating force for human activities.

The need of a futuristic moneyless society, as proposed by the Zeitgeist Movement, may be a long term, concrete utopia, but a short term step of gradually depending less on the fee-per-service culture, and more on service according to need and contribution according to abilities ideology, as Karl Marx proposed, is a progressive way to a more egalitarian society. For example a fare-free city transit, a comprehensive, universal, free of charge health care system, etc.

7. 8 - **A Matter of Priorities.**

We often hear from politicians and the media that the government can not afford to maintain the social services we need. Their reasons for austerity are usually an economic crisis, an economic recession, or just scarcity of money.

Two facts about money of which we must be clear:

First - The economy is not the wealthy provider of social services; the economy is nothing more than an accounting system of transactions. The rules of this accounting system are regulated by tax laws.

Therefore, politicians, in theory, have the responsibility to legislate the collection of as much financial resources as required to provide the best possible social services. If fair and sufficient taxes were collected, no deficits would ever ensue.

However, in practice politicians following the business agenda, instead of collecting enough taxes to balance with the need to fund social services, they legislate reducing or exempting taxes from high earning individuals and from businesses.

Tax cuts obviously create budget deficits and consequently reduction of services. We, the majority of citizens, not a few politicians, need to decide the taxes we pay and the budgets for each ministry.

Second - Most politicians have agreed that we need more social services, "If only we could afford them".

At the same time however, a few business consultants and a few politicians often prioritize expensive projects, which are profitable to business, instead of financing social services.

We must be clear that poor social services in our society are a matter poor government's priorities, not a lack of people's money.

"The only way in which radical change can be conceived today is not as the taking of power but as the dissolution of [centralized] power."
John Holloway

7.9 - Once we realize the imminent need for social change, the first concrete step is to clearly define the people's agenda and write it down into a citizens constitution.

The hope is that as a few of us start participating in PDD it will inspire other citizens to perceive their tangible power. Once citizens realize that their input is registered, discussed, and counted, once it is realized that they can genuinely influence the outcome of our collective political decisions, their interest in political participation will also increase.

The Jewish Scholar Hillel
(60 BC - 10 AD) said:
"If not now, when?"

Now is the time because we still have the ability to find a relatively painless change to avoid the predicted economic and ecological catastrophe, because that is where our current political system is headed.

CHAPTER 8

Resistance to change

The human brain struggles between emotion and reason. The fears of change from the known to the unknown, coupled with the comfortable feelings from a routine living often eclipses rational need for change from the traditional to a new system.

Historically, social changes like banning child labour, civil rights to abolish segregation, and to allow women to vote in North America took many decades to be realized and successfully adopted.

These cultural symptoms continue to affect our political evolution. Even if many of us recognize our readiness and ability to make our own political decisions, many others prefer to hold on to the tradition of representative democracy.

Delegating social responsibility to a few political representatives becomes seemingly more convenient to our busy lives. It gives us an illusion of democracy and a relief from the responsibilities of making political decisions.

In this chapter we address a few common excuses people use to avoid participating on social issues. This cultural resistance to change comes from apathy, insecurity, and cynicism.

8.1 - Job Insecurity.

One of the objections many people have to the existing BC "Recall and Initiative Legislation", a rudimentary precursor to PDD, is the concern that recalling politicians may bring an unfair job insecurity to politicians, and consequently we would fail to attract the best educated and trained people to legislate our polices.

Addressing the concern of unfairness to politicians, we must remember that recalling faulty consumer goods is a frequent affair, and although it might be economically detrimental to manufactures, recalling of any product is a well accepted as a consumers' right. Furthermore, dismissing professionals, trade workers, and public or private employees for their unacceptable   performance is also a commonly practiced labour standard. So, even if recalling politicians may not appear to be fair to them, politicians deserve equal labour rights treatment.

The financial security of a politician who suddenly loses a political office, needs to be fairly compensated through government employment benefits, available to all public employees.

Addressing the concern of "attracting the best qualified citizens for the political job", we may consider the proposition of this PDD thesis, and more specifically the suggestion of the Citizen's Constitution on chapter 7. That is, when we the citizens, become legislators of our own laws, political executives do not need to be extraordinary leaders. Politicians simply need to properly follow the will of the electorate, not as leaders, but as administrators, or executive managers of government.

Ultimately, to make politicians truly accountable to citizens, we must have the right and the ability to recall them.

8.2 - Public Forums "Yes" - Recall "No".

Many progressive thinkers support, in principle, the idea of public forums, but do not support the voter's right to recall politicians; implying that punishing a few politicians may not change the unwanted government's policies.

Although this conclusion may be true under the current representative party system, it is not so under PDD, the fact remains that voting for politicians and voting for policy issues are two sides of the same coin. On the one side is the people's choice of politicians, on the other side is the people's choice of laws, or bylaws; therefore, recalling an elected official and recalling a specific government policy are the same expression of the peoples' right to choose.

Supporting public forums is obviously fundamental. Factual information and discussion period are essential to democracy, but it should not preclude the voter's right to recall politicians. One action does not cancel or contradict the other. In principle, they are complementary and the same voter's right.

8.3 - Political Stability.

Critics of PDD often comment that, "Politicians need a term of office to accomplish legislative work." And that, "perpetual recall" would paralyze government work because politicians would be too busy, always looking over their shoulder, and perpetually campaigning to be re-elected.

If politicians are recalled while controversial legislation is being discussed, or before the completion of a project, we should question the politician's decision and the project itself, rather than the citizens right to recall the politician in order to stop an unwanted decision. Entrusting politicians with the absolute legal authority to make any political decisions, regardless of whether the electorate agrees with it or not, during a term of office, is in fact, signing a blank cheque for any purpose. It legally means tying up the citizens' hands, and letting politicians do almost whatever they please during their term of office. The right to recall makes politicians accountable to their constituents.

8.4 - For how long should we live with our mistakes?

It is understandable to hear politicians, who are potentially affected by recall-legislation, say: "voters should live with their mistaken choice till the next election." What is most puzzling to hear is ordinary people advocating to punish themselves, for a term of 3 or 4 years, for a mistaken choice, made on one election day.

It is reasonable to expect that people will make electoral mistakes, by voting on quick reactions, or momentary emotional impulses, as we get saturated with media propaganda and misinformation at the last moment of casting our vote.

However, this human vulnerability, should not be the reason to punish ourselves to suffer the consequences of our mistake for years before we can rectify it, ironically when we have the computer technology available to recast our vote and potentially rectify any mistaken decisions instantly.

8.5 - Ambiguous Context - Skewed Results.

Another common objection to referendum reasonably argues that the wording of the referendum questions as well as the context of the question are often skewed and convoluted enough to produce a leading or unintended outcome.

Referendum questions, usually written by highly educated teams of lawyers, can often be ambiguous and confusing. An example of a convoluted question was the 2011 HST referendum in BC where "Yes" meant to reject HST and "NO" meant to accept HST.

Seth Klein, director of the Centre for Canadian Policy Alternatives in BC, explains how important the context of a question can be, by noting that if people are asked: "Do you want to pay more taxes?" most people are going to say "No", but when the question includes a context like: "Do you want to increase your taxes in order to improve your health care services?" most people have unequivocally answered "Yes".

One solution, to deal with the wording and the context of a referendum question, is presented by a pilot project at www.nowpolling.ca, where the citizens' initiatives or questions, are written by the citizens themselves, in their own words, with their own context. The proposed Citizens' Constitution, on the next chapter, also suggests that, the formulating of a referendum questions should not come from an exclusive elite, but it should be originated from all the citizens themselves.

8.6- Ignorant People Don't Know Better.

The most common objection to PDD suggests that people do not know better, and therefore, when ignorant people are given the right to decide, they will shoot themselves in the foot.

The often cited case is Proposition 13 of the Constitution of the State of California, a People's Initiative to Limit Property Taxation. The successful proposition decreased property taxes, bringing as a consequence, the inevitable and drastic reduction of public services. Obviously, most Californians were not fully aware of the self-inflicting effects of reducing taxes.

An initiative must be followed by as much factual information about the topic as possible, and a reasonable amount of time for public discussion, should be allowed before the final referendum is executed.

After the public is well informed, and a discussion period has been allowed, the referendum question can not be postponed indefinitely. A decision must be enacted.

The issue in this case is not whether voters select their best choice; the issues we need to investigate here are: first - was there sufficient factual information available? second - was there sufficient time allowed for discussion? and third - do citizens have the right and the ability to rectify their mistaken votes if they change their mind? PDD as demonstrated on www.nowpolling.ca offers a potential approach to these issues.

8.7 - Media Brainwashing.

Many Social Democrats in Canada argue that "PDD" in the context of mass media being owned and operated by businesses' interests, will be easily co-opted to serve as a tool for those with the financial resources to direct it.

Matthew Robinson expands on this issue in his book, "Mobocracy: How the Media's Obsession with Polling Twists the News, Alters Elections, and Undermines Democracy."

This influential phenomenon of media may appear to be insurmountable and convincing, but If we believe that we are trapped between a conspiring elite, and a brainless mob, then there is no hope for the evolution of democracy. However, if we choose to believe in with a "concrete utopia", as Economist Ingo Schmidt explained, we don't abandon our dreams in desperation, instead, we optimistically participate in the planning of possible solutions or "concrete utopias" then we can overcome the media propaganda.

8.8 - Can Politicians Prejudice Themselves?

Politicians are One of the obstacles for change. Former politician himself Gordon Gibson explained that because politicians are the gate keepers of political change, recall and referendum would be in detrimental conflict with their self interests. Understandably, they want to keep the political power in their own hands, and therefore they are generally not interested in changing the very system which authorizes them to rule from above.

8.9 - Can Democracy Be Too Expensive?

Many politicians accept, in principle, the idea of PDD; however, they quickly dismiss it as too expensive. Victoria Mayor Dean Fortin told me recently that a single referendum question could cost the city up to $200.000. I pointed out to him that the www.nowpolling.ca computerized initiative and plebiscite system cost us less than $1,000.

Considering that general elections cost each city an average of $10 million dollars every three years, it is reasonable to think that a computerized electoral system, perpetually open to the citizens in existing libraries and community centres, could cost the same or less than the present system.

Finally, we must be aware that federal politicians who object to extending power to the people continue gradually delegating their financial and international trading authority to transnational business associations at the same time under "Free Trade Agreements," and financial and monetary cartels. This has been clearly demonstrated by the U.S. Federal Reserve Bank and more recently shown by the managers of the "Euro," ruling from above.

This dependency on a hierarchical chain of command, where most politicians only play a token role of leadership is explained by **Nick Cowen in his** book "Total Recall" where he shows how U.K. politicians have slowly ceded their powers to a few ministers, government agencies and the European Union.

CHAPTER 9

Citizen's Draft Constitution.

With the intention of advancing a peaceful evolution of democracy, we, the concerned citizens, volunteer to participate in the development of an evolving constitution.

To begin the perpetual process of direct democracy, we present the following initiatives, a set of suggestions to develop a political framework, not as an accomplished fact, but as a perpetual democratic process, for your consideration.

You can participate with your own initiatives, amendments, or rejection of any of the following propositions on   www.nowpolling.ca , or your can add your vote of support for some of the initiatives already posted.

An initiative proposition, after allowing a predetermined and sufficient time for full information and public discussion, may be qualified as a binding referendum, and when approved by a predetermined threshold of majority, it shall be amended into law. All statutes in this constitution are mutable. All laws and policies may be amended anytime.

Motion #1: Empathy, (Love)

- Because an ideal social consciousness evolves from cooperation, fairness, and restorative justice;
- Because empathy is our natural ability to feel the joys and pains of others.
- Because the well-being of others is interconnected with our well-being.
- Therefore, all Laws written in this constitution, must indispensably harmonize with the Spirit of Empathy as embodied in the Universal Charter of Rights and Freedoms, and in any other document made with the intention to protect collective and individual human rights.

Motion #2: Equality and Freedom

- Because equality and freedom are fundamental human values;
- Because hierarchy and competition create social, economic, and political inequality;
- Therefore, we declare to be sovereign from any hierarchical authority and commit ourselves to cooperate within the principle of equality, among ourselves and with other societies.

Motion #3: Justice and Peace

- Because although war and aggression may bring order, it does not bring a Just peace,
- Because the security of one is the security of all.
- Therefore, we the citizens commit ourselves to research, develop, and practice the theories of restorative justice and nonviolent conflict resolution, among ourselves and with other nations.

Motion #4: Ecological Conservation.

- Because we live in a world of limited resources,
- Because all life is imperiled by the extraction, manufacturing, and use of toxic elements,
-Therefore, we must consciously regulate the rate of mining toxic elements, the creation of life threatening products, and the consumption of harmful and scarce resources.

Motion #5. - Territorial Coexistence

- Recognizing that the citizens' perception of democracy ,and the citizens' choice of priorities within a common territory may be diverse and sometimes conflicting,
- Considering that a respectful and orderly coexistence, among different ethnic and cultural nations residing in a common territory, is an essential factor for a democratic society, and

- in view of the emerging PDD political system, which is distinct from the current Representative Democracy.
- Therefore, we the citizens, constituents of PDD, and residents of this territory, now known as (name of province, state, or geographical boundaries), agree to negotiate, with the existing political representatives and governments, a mutually acceptable set of regulations and agreements conducive to an orderly and peaceful coexistence.

Motion #6. - Community Associations

Community associations are groups of a reasonable number of citizens of a neighborhood who can identify their common interests, discuss their initiatives, and tabulate their plebiscites.

The shared consensus of the group should be intertwined, as an interactive and interdependent legislation, into Municipal departments, into Provincial / State Ministries, and into the Federal Government of Canada.

Motion #7. - Municipal Governments.

7.1 - City Governments are administered by elected City Executive Officers.

7.2 .- City Executive Officers shall be elected by the constituents of all Community Associations within the city through a perpetual electoral system operated by the city's Legislative Operations Department.

7.3 - The duty of each City Executive Officer shall be to implement the citizens decisions, and to manage an assigned department of the municipality as mandated.

7.4 - The number of departments and the number of executive officers elected for each department on each city, shall be decided by its citizens, depending on the size of their constituency and according to the people's perceived need.

7.5 - City Executive Officers shall present a yearly financial budget for their department. Budgets need to be approved by referendum by the majority of electorates.

7.6 - Example List of municipal departments,
    a) - Legislative operations, Elections, Initiative and Referendum.
    b) - Public Information and Communications Systems.

c) - Public Works: Water, sewer, garbage, recycling.

d) - City Planning, street works, and Building permits

e) - Social services, Parks and Recreation.

f) - Social Housing and Public Transit.

g) - Credit Management Agency:
Tax collection and funding distribution.

h) - Police; Law enforcement, public security.

i) - Inter governmental coordination.

7.7 - Each department shall operate according to a mandate described under a People's Municipal Act.

Motion #8. - Provincial or State Government

8.1 - The Provincial or State Government shall be Administered by elected Executive State Ministers.

8.2. - Executive ministers shall be elected "at large" by all citizens across the state by a perpetual electoral system.

8.3 - The electoral system shall be operated by the Ministry of Citizens' Legislation.

8.4 - Citizens may decide to have more than one executive minister for any ministry, in that case, the top two, or more elected candidates would become a committee of ministers, for a particular ministry.

8.5. - The Ministers' duty shall be to introduce and implement legislation as decided by citizens, and to administer government's operations, in accordance with the laws and statutes mandated by the citizens.

8.6. - Ministers shall present, to the electorate, a yearly financial budget for their assigned ministry. This shall be discussed by the citizens and approved by referendum.

8.7 - Sample list of Ministries:

a) - Ministry of the Premier

The Premier's duty is: to assist other ministers with the Legislation of citizens' initiatives decided by referendum, to symbolically represent the State, nationally and internationally. the Premier shall comply with all the statutes in accordance with a State's Governance Act.

b) - Ministry of Citizens' Legislation

The Ministry of Citizens' Legislation shall develop and operate a computerized, perpetual polling system to facilitate citizens' initiative, referendum, and the elections of ministers. This Ministry must ensure that the polling system is secure, transparent, verifiable, and accessible to all citizens, every business day. The Minister shall comply with all the statues within a Citizens' Legislation Act.

c) - Ministry of Attorney General/Justice.
The Ministry of the Attorney General shall mange the legal procedures of creating new bills for the implementation of peoples' legislation into law; the Minister shall safe-keep the laws and constitution; the Attorney General is the Chief Executive Officer of the Justice and Courts System; and the Minister shall comply with all the statutes of a Justice Act.

d) - Ministry of Finance
The Ministry of Finance shall administer the collection of taxes and other revenues from citizens, and businesses; the ministry of Finance shall administer the distribution of financial resources to all ministries according to their budgets, and according to the statutes in a Finance Act.

e) Ministry of Currency and Credit.
the Ministry shall manage a credit agency to create the capital needed for building infrastructure projects.

f) Ministry of Health Care.

The Ministry of Health Care shall operate a non-profit, efficient, comprehensive, universal, and sufficiently available to all, health care and health prevention service.

g) Ministry of Education

The Ministry of Education shall operate an efficient, non-profit, skill trades, academic, kindergarden to university educational services, sufficiently available to all, and fully financed by taxes.

h) Ministry of Housing.

The Ministry of Housing shall, in coordination with regional, federal, and non-profit social housing agencies, develop, maintain, and manage sufficient housing for all citizens who need it.

i) Ministry of Transportation.

The Ministry of Transportation, in coordination with municipal transit authorities and federal funding programs, shall develop infrastructure, purchase equipment and operate not-for profit transit services, as needed by citizens.

j) Ministry of Communications & Information.

The Ministry of Communications and Information shall regulate the communications systems; gather and publish, relevant information from all ministries, and keep archival records and vital statistics. Freedom of information and individual privacy rights should be applied accordingly.

k) Ministry of Social Services/Welfare

The Ministry of Social Services and Welfare in conjunction with municipal social services and federal projects shall develop and operate public services to aid low income, elders, infirm, drug addicted, and mentally challenged citizens.

L) Ministry of the Solicitor General

The Ministry of the Solicitor General, in coordination with the municipal police units, shall provide public security and order; it shall administer detention centers. Detention centers shall develop and provide restorative justice training, and non-violence conflict resolution training, in coordination with the education ministry.

m) Ministry of Forest-Lands-Minerals.

This Ministry shall regulate and manage all public lands prioritizing the optimum ecological sustainability and to the most public benefit possible.

n) Ministry of Food Security & Agriculture.

This Ministry shall regulate food production, distribution, and safety.

o) Ministry of Energy

This Ministry shall regulate the production and distribution of energy from all sources: gas, oil, hydro, wind, tidal, solar, etc.

p) Ministry of Business & Labour.

This Ministry shall regulate all business procedures and obligations, labour rights and safety conditions.

q) Ministry of Intergovernmental Affairs

The purpose of this ministry is to constantly negotiate our economic and social responsibilities with municipalities and regional governments, as well as our political commitments and obligations within our sovereign states and internationally.

Motion #9
Governance of the Federation of Canada

9.1 - The governance of the Federation of Canada needs to be re-negotiated between those provinces which would want to continue to elect representative legislators to parliament, and the new sovereign state(s) which would chose citizens's legislation as agreed in the PDD system.

9.2 PDD State(s) would delegate Executive Ministers to Co-administer each Federal Ministry.

9.3. - From a list of candidates across the State for each federal ministry, an Executive Co-Minister shall be elected for each ministry and delegated to the Canadian Government in Ottawa.

9.4 - Citizens may decide to have more than one federal Co Minister for any Ministry, in that case, the top two, or more elected candidates would become a committee of ministers, for a particular ministry.

9.5 - The Co-Ministers' mandate shall last as long as the majority of citizens across the province maintain the public support for them, on the official - computerized - perpetual electoral system.

9.6 - The federal Co-Ministers' foremost duty shall be to negotiate, with other Ministers of other federated states or provinces of the Canadian Government, bills of legislation as decided by the electorates, and second, to ensure that their specific ministries execute operations as mandated.

9.7 - Each Federal Co-Minister from each State or province, shall present a yearly financial budget for their ministry. All federal budgets need to be decided by referendum by the taxpayers of each State or province.

9.8 - If a super majority of at least 67% of citizens of any State or province object to any decision by the Canadian Parliament, that State or Province, shall not be obliged to contribute financially nor participate on that parliament's decision.

9.9 - An example List of Federal Ministries, which citizens of of this Sovereign State, (province) may want to participate in, and delegate   a Co-Minister for each ministry.

a).-Ministry of Information, Initiative, and Plebiscite.

b).- Ministry of the Prime Minister.

c).- Ministry of Justice, Attorney General

d).- Ministry of Health Care Services

e).- Ministry of Intergovernmental Internal Affairs

f).- Ministry of Foreign Affairs

g).- Ministry of Defense and training for Natural disasters aid and rescue.

h).- Ministry for the Environmental protection.

i).- Ministry for Nonviolent conflict resolution training.

j).- Ministry of Finance

k).- Ministry of Food Security and Agriculture.

l).- Ministry of Social Services

m).- Ministry of Communications and Transportation Infrastructure.

n).- Ministry of International Trade.

o).- Ministry of Labour and business regulations

p).- Ministry of Immigration

q).- Ministry of Natural Resources and Energy.

Epilogue

This PDD thesis attempts not just to show the pitfalls of our present political system, but it offers a potential new political system within the framework of a Citizen's Constitution.

It suggests that statutory changes and constitutional laws need to resonate and harmonize with a Citizen's needs. It also suggests a shift from a system based in political and economic competition, where money begetting money is the motivation of human activities, into a new system where providing social services becomes the collective responsibility and the main purpose of society.

This PDD framework is not a monolithic program to be literally followed. It is only a set of observations and practical suggestions in the midst of our precarious time. The easiest thing is to dismiss it and do nothing. By default one becomes a passive observer; however, we can chose to be active participants in changing our social system,

We must keep in mind that by participating with our individual opinions for examination, discussion, and tabulation, on an established official poll, we will inevitably contribute in the production of a higher social consciousness.

So far, this booklet offers the opinions of a small number of participants on www.nowpolling.ca; therefore the results are not yet significant, however, since our cultural hegemony is always in flux, PDD is suggested as a small starting contribution to perhaps a larger long term solution.

As the longest walk starts with one step, every one of us can start to swing the pendulum of politics away from cynicism and apathy, and move it towards citizens creating, shaping, and building the public good which our communities need.

"Self-determination[PDD] is inherently uncertain. The death of the old certainties is to be welcomed as a liberation." John Holloway

ABOUT THE AUTHOR

The author is a father and grandfather who lives with his wife in Victoria, Canada

He is a retired videographer who manages a polling system on: www.nowpolling.ca and is associated with a video productions collective that webcast on www.pasifik.ca

You can contact the author through either of the above websites

www.ingramcontent.com/pod-product-compliance
Lightning Source LLC
Chambersburg PA
CBHW060204290526
45789CB00003B/1153